DOGS SET VI

MASTIFFS

Nancy Furstinger
ABDO Publishing Company

**visit us at
www.abdopub.com**

Published by ABDO Publishing Company, 4940 Viking Drive, Edina, Minnesota 55435.
Copyright © 2006 by Abdo Consulting Group, Inc. International copyrights reserved in
all countries. No part of this book may be reproduced in any form without written
permission from the publisher. The Checkerboard Library™ is a trademark and logo of
ABDO Publishing Company.

Printed in the United States.

Cover Photo: Animals Animals
Interior Photos: AP/Wide World pp. 17, 19; Corbis pp. 5, 7, 8, 9, 11, 15, 16, 21; Getty
    Images p. 13; Peter Arnold p. 20

Series Coordinator: Megan M. Gunderson
Editors: Megan M. Gunderson, Megan Murphy
Art Direction: Neil Klinepier

Library of Congress Cataloging-in-Publication Data

Furstinger, Nancy.
    Mastiffs / Nancy Furstinger.
        p. cm. -- (Dogs. Set VI)
    Includes bibliographical references and index.
    ISBN 1-59679-273-6
    1. Mastiff breeds--Juvenile literature. I. Title.

    SF429.M36F87 2005
    636.73--dc22

                                                    2005042128

CONTENTS

THE DOG FAMILY

Thousands of years ago, people welcomed wolf pups as pets, hunters, and guards. These pups were among the first animals that humans tamed. These pets developed into **domestic** dogs. Now more than 12,000 years later, dogs are often our best friends.

Almost 400 different **breeds** of dogs exist worldwide. These dogs vary in appearance. They range from pocket- to pony-sized. Some have been bred for special purposes, such as guarding property or pulling carts.

Despite their differences, all dogs belong to the Canidae **family**. This name comes from the Latin word *canis*, which means "dog." The Canidae family also includes wolves, coyotes, foxes, and jackals.

These shaggy dogs all belong to the Canidae family.

Dogs and wolves are still similar in many ways. Both communicate through howling and growling. They mark their territory and have well-developed senses of smell and hearing.

MASTIFFS

Mastiffs may have originated in parts of Asia, such as Tibet and northern India. Large dogs similar to mastiffs are mentioned in the documents and legends of cultures across the world.

Giant dogs similar to mastiffs also lived in Europe as far back as 3000 BC. Foreign traders probably brought these dogs to Great Britain more than 2,000 years ago. There, this ancient **breed** guarded homes and cattle.

These big, brave dogs also fought in many wars. But, the mastiff's courage was often misused. Mastiffs were pitted against human gladiators. They fought bears, bulls, lions, and tigers, as well as other dogs.

In 1885, the mastiff **breed** was recognized by the **American Kennel Club (AKC)**. Mastiffs were popular in England, too. But, they nearly disappeared before **World War I**. Fortunately, this breed is popular once again.

Mastiffs battled other dogs in London's Westminster Pit as late as the 1900s.

What They're Like

A book from the year 1800 describes the mastiff's personality. "What the lion is to the cat, the mastiff is to the dog, the noblest of the family." Today, this **breed**'s courage, dignity, and good nature continue to win it praise.

Mastiffs are sensitive souls. They are sometimes referred to as "gentle giants." They need to be **socialized** to keep from becoming too

As of 2005, Neapolitan mastiffs such as this one can compete in AKC dog shows.

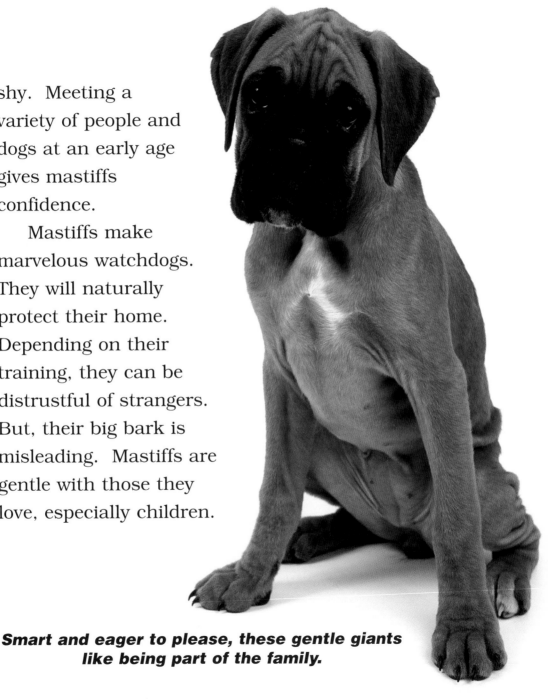

shy. Meeting a variety of people and dogs at an early age gives mastiffs confidence.

Mastiffs make marvelous watchdogs. They will naturally protect their home. Depending on their training, they can be distrustful of strangers. But, their big bark is misleading. Mastiffs are gentle with those they love, especially children.

Smart and eager to please, these gentle giants like being part of the family.

COAT AND COLOR

The mastiff has a coarse outer coat. This straight hair is short. It shields a short, thick undercoat.

The coat comes in three colors. The apricot and silver fawn coats are shades of light brown and white. The brindle pattern has an apricot or fawn background color covered with dark streaks.

All mastiffs have dark **muzzles**, ears, and noses. This darker color also circles the eyes. Some dogs also have a small patch of white on the chest.

Opposite page: *This mastiff shows the dark muzzle and black nose required by the AKC. In 2004, more than 6,000 mastiffs were registered with the AKC.*

SIZE

The mastiff is a large **breed**. Males stand at least 30 inches (76 cm) high at the shoulders. Females stand more than 27 inches (69 cm) high. Mastiffs weigh an average of 175 to 190 pounds (80 to 85 kg).

In 1989, a mastiff named Zorba appeared in *The Guinness Book of World Records* as the world's largest dog. He weighed an amazing 343 pounds (156 kg)! And, Zorba measured 99 inches (251 cm) from his nose to the tip of his tail.

The mastiff is built for strength. These dogs have powerful muscles and a rectangular body. They have a wrinkled forehead and a broad skull that is slightly flat between the ears. The **muzzle** is blunt, and their lips hang down on either side.

Mastiffs have dark brown eyes that are set wide apart. Their ears are V-shaped with rounded tips. The mastiff's wide tail tapers at the end and hangs straight.

This male mastiff named Butch weighed more than 200 pounds (90 kg)! Females generally weigh less than males.

CARE

The mastiff's short coat is simple to groom.
Still, this **breed**'s massive size means that you'll
need to spend more time brushing. Use a dog glove
or a short-bristled brush. These grooming tools are
well suited for the mastiff's short fur.

Every mastiff sheds a little differently. Some
shed all year. Others shed in spring and fall. And,
some mastiffs shed their short, fine undercoat in
the summer months. However, mastiffs will shed
very little if brushed daily.

Owners should also check daily to make sure
the ears, eyes, and lips stay clean. And, a mastiff's
teeth should be brushed regularly. Owners can use
a soft-bristled brush and a toothpaste made
specifically for dogs.

A dog should visit a veterinarian each year. At that time, a mastiff will receive a health checkup and **vaccines**. A veterinarian can also help owners decide whether to **spay** or **neuter** a pet.

Unlike most dogs, mastiffs should not be bathed very often. To prevent skin problems, only bathe your mastiff when it is very dirty or when it is going to be in a dog show.

FEEDING

Mastiff puppies weigh only one pound (.5 kg) at birth. But, they grow at an amazing rate! For this reason, puppies need to eat the right food.

Eating small meals several times a day will help this giant **breed** grow at a slow and steady pace. This way, your mastiff will develop into a healthy dog. A breeder or veterinarian can help recommend a balanced diet.

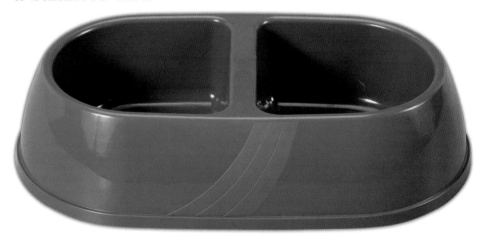

For food and water, most dogs can use hard plastic dishes like this one. But because of their powerful jaws, mastiffs should use dishes made of a stronger material such as stainless steel.

Many stores offer healthy pet food. Some stores even allow your dog inside the store with you!

Despite their enormous size, mastiffs eat about the same amount as other large **breeds**. Still, watch your mastiff's weight. Excess weight can cause bone, joint, and other health problems.

Fill a big, stainless steel bowl with fresh, clean water. Your mastiff will dribble after it drinks and eats. So, keep a towel handy to wipe the drool.

Mastiffs adore chewing. They need large, strong chew toys. Playthings made especially for big breeds should stand up to their powerful jaws.

THINGS THEY NEED

Surprisingly, mastiffs don't need a lot of exercise. This **breed** should avoid brisk exercise until they are at least 18 months old. Their bodies are still growing. Too much exercise will stress their bones and muscles.

Training is an important part of raising a dog. During daily walks, practice heeling. This is when a dog follows or moves along close to someone. Walks should be short at first. But as a mastiff ages, the walks can become longer.

Make training a fun game. Use a pleasant but firm voice, and keep lessons short. Reward the dog with treats and praise. Mastiffs are intelligent and will respond well to consistent training.

Decide on the first day whether your mastiff can climb up on the furniture. Keep in mind that your small puppy will soon weigh around 150 pounds (68 kg). And, establish a specific place for your mastiff's dog bed. Beware, most mastiffs snore!

Remember to attach a tag with your dog's name, address, and phone number to its collar. This is important in case your dog ever becomes lost.

PUPPIES

Search for a veterinarian before you bring your new mastiff home. A breeder can recommend one in the area for you.

Mastiffs are pregnant for about nine weeks. Large **breeds** can give birth to up to ten or twelve puppies in each **litter**.

Mastiff puppies are blind and deaf at birth. At first, they spend their time sleeping, eating, and

Many different breeds can make good family dogs.

cuddling together. They open their eyes and ears after about two weeks. Puppies take their first steps at three weeks.

Puppies are usually **weaned** by seven weeks of age. They develop their true colors by eight weeks. And, they can be adopted when they are between eight and twelve weeks old.

Search for a qualified **breeder** if you want to purchase a **purebred** mastiff. A breed rescue or the **Humane Society** may have mastiff puppies and older dogs for adoption.

Puppies get their first series of shots when they are between six and eight weeks old. After you bring your new mastiff home, the veterinarian will give them more **vaccines** and check for worms. A healthy mastiff will live about eight to ten years.

GLOSSARY

American Kennel Club (AKC) - an organization that studies and promotes interest in purebred dogs.

breed - a group of animals sharing the same appearance and characteristics. A breeder is a person who raises animals. Raising animals is often called breeding them.

domestic - animals that are tame.

family - a group that scientists use to classify similar plants or animals. It ranks above a genus and below an order.

Humane Society - an organization that protects and cares for animals.

litter - all of the puppies born at one time to a mother dog.

muzzle - an animal's nose and jaws.

neuter (NOO-tuhr) - to remove a male animal's reproductive organs.

purebred - an animal whose parents are both from the same breed.

socialize - to accustom an animal or person to spending time with others.

spay - to remove a female animal's reproductive organs.

vaccine (vak-SEEN) - a shot given to animals or humans to prevent them from getting an illness or disease.

wean - to accustom an animal to eat food other than its mother's milk.

World War I - from 1914 to 1918, fought in Europe. Great Britain, France, Russia, the United States, and their allies were on one side. Germany, Austria-Hungary, and their allies were on the other side.

WEB SITES

To learn more about mastiffs, visit ABDO Publishing Company on the World Wide Web at **www.abdopub.com**. Web sites about mastiffs are featured on our Book Links page. These links are routinely monitored and updated to provide the most current information available.

INDEX